LOOKING INSIDE

Life Lessons From a Multiple Personality

In Pictures and Words
Second Edition

Judy Castelli

Universal Publishers / uPUBLISH.com
USA • 2001
ISBN 1-58112-682-4
www.upublish.com/books/castelli.htm

Second Edition
Looking Inside is also available in e-book format.

This book was originally published by:
Castelli Studios, East Hampton, NY, August, 2000

Also available by the author:
The DID Journal Kit: For Therapists and People with
Multiple Personality and Dissociative Identity Disorder

For further information, speaking engagements,
or press packet:

Visit us on the WEB:
www.multiple-personality.com

Castelli Studios
211 Buckskill Road, East Hampton, NY 11937
Phone: 631-329-3813
Fax: 631-329-2842

DEDICATION

Our thanks to all who have not seen, yet they believe.

TABLE OF CONTENTS

FOREWORD

By Judy Castelli

From age eighteen to age forty-four, I spent many weeks and months in psychiatric hospitals. I received anti-psychotic medications, anti-depressants, lithium, seizure medications, and anti-anxiety medications. I took them, in various combinations, hoping for relief from the constant screaming in my head.

There were voices that told me I was "BAD." There were voices that told me to "DIE." There were voices that told me to cut out my eyes, and voices that told me to set myself on fire. I lived with the constant threat of suicide. I looked, acted, and felt crazy. I *was* crazy.

On the verge of a contract with a major record label, I abandoned my dream of becoming a singer/songwriter. My artwork appeased my creative juices, while for fifteen years, I worked with a wonderful and caring psychotherapist, and I was healing.

I eventually 'graduated' therapy. My diagnosis was still schizophrenia, and I was still taking medications, but during good periods, I was able to sustain work. I was in a loving supportive relationship, and I was happy.

In 1994, I opened a stained glass studio in the same Day Treatment Center where I had been a patient twenty years prior. I hired and trained ten people with mental illness to build my Tiffany Style lamps. We all worked part time, and sold the lamps we made to Bloomingdale's in New York. I was doing well.

The responsibility of running the business was intense. I was starting to feel un-well. Flashes of memory disturbed my daily life. I called my former therapist and asked if she could squeeze me in. I was "not okay." She saw me on her lunch hour. A little bit into the session, she asked if I could tell her what was going on. I said I really didn't know. For some reason, she said these words, "Perhaps some other part of you knows."

The response came from my lips in a voice that was not mine. "Torture." This was the personality we would call Gravely Voice.

Without further invitation, seven other alter-personalities came forward to tell what they knew. They used my vocal chords, my throat, my body, and they were not me. They were telling the secret that they had kept hidden for a lifetime: child abuse. My life turned upside down, and changed forever.

My therapist said that she thought they had misdiagnosed me from the beginning. This "appeared to be" a dissociative disorder, but she had no experience with DID. She would call her friend who was an expert. I would go home and wait. I don't remember how I got home.

For the next eight days, I was flooded with memories of horrific childhood abuse. My child alters relived the original trauma in my adult body. Alters seemed to be coming out of the woodwork. I couldn't control any of it.

The DID "expert" suggested to my therapist, that if I was already having "body-memories", I needed to be in a hospital with a specialty in Dissociative Identity Disorders, preferably one with a separate DID unit. There were only eight in the country at the time. She called them all. I would take the first one that had a bed.

In November of 1994, I was diagnosed with Dissociative Identity Disorder (Multiple Personality Disorder). I have forty-four alter-personalities.

Dissociative Identity Disorder often looks like many other mental disorders, including schizophrenia. I suffered most of my adult life due to ignorance of DID, and I am grateful that I was finally diagnosed correctly.

This hospitalization at Northwestern Institute was painful, yet healing. Upon release, I began therapy with Renee' Hoffman, C.S.W., who had extensive experience working with trauma survivors. I returned to the hospital twice more to deal with alters who had reverted to fire, and thoughts of suicide.

Together, the personalities would have to find new ways to deal with the reality of my childhood, the memories, and life with Multiple Personality Disorder.

After one of my first sessions with my doctor at Northwestern, I cornered her in the hall. I asked her to explain how this was supposed to work. How was I supposed to get better?

The flashbacks had not stopped, I was switching constantly, and I was losing time, and had amnesia of events and conversation. I was in total chaos, and I was frightened. "Ask inside," she said. "Ask, who needs to talk." Moving quickly down the hall, she turned back to me and added, "Journal!"

I started immediately. Telling the secrets was just the first step to ending the pain. We would have to understand this complex system of alter personalities and get them all working together. The answers were inside. We intended to survive the memories, and the speaking of the truth. We would have to heal from the inside out. *This is what Bob means.*

My journals saved my life. There, all parts of the mind could freely express whatever was inside, whatever they needed to say. We tried not to censor, not to judge.

I am pleased to offer the drawings and text on these pages, taken directly from my journals. Not poetry. But the words sometimes read like poetry. They illustrate the struggles, the joys, the mystery, the wonder, the ups and downs, the ins and outs of life with multiplicity.

Renee', Phyllis, and my friends at The New York Society for the Study of Multiple Personality and Dissociation, have been marvelous supports. My Website, www.multiple-personality.com keeps me connected with other Multiples, their loved ones, and professionals working in the field.

I am doing well. I am fully functioning as a Multiple. I am almost completely "co-conscious," and there are no parts of me who want to hurt or kill the body we share. I have been free of medications for over five years.

this is my goal

If there is tragedy here, it is in the abuse of a child- a child unseen. The effects of child abuse last a lifetime. Nevertheless, with the correct diagnosis and proper treatment, recovery is possible. You can heal yourself, from the inside out.

With the diagnosis of Multiple Personality / Dissociative Identity Disorder, I was given a chance at a new life. The chaos that was my life is over. I am still healing. I am still Multiple, but I am whole, and I am happy.

This is a world that does not see its' children, and does not care to know. There is hope in these pages for all who suffer still, and for those who are alone in a world that is hard on anyone different. Multiple is different.

I invite you all, to look inside.

WE BEGIN

Taking the Leap.

Trusting there will be stars.

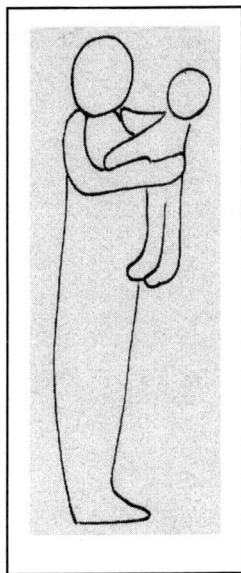

I wake up calling for Mommy.

It's a Little One.

We're just little.

Not scared.

Sad.

It's funny how things are turning out in this life.

It's not what I had thought.

I am lost.

How do I get from here to there?

I am blind.

No eyes to see.

I take another

step.

Another.

I climb the

mountain

in darkness.

The next step

will kill me.

If I do not see it,

I will not know.

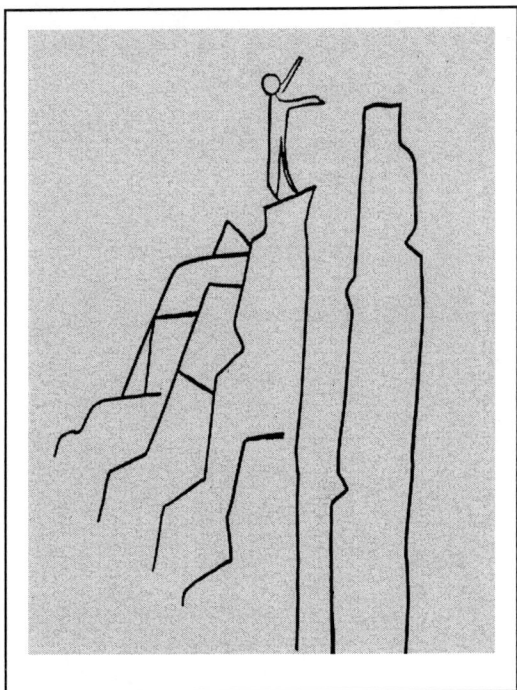

If I see I will not dare to make the leap.

Either way, I do not win this game.

There is no prize for winning.

I do not expect to win.

You will survive this night.

We have survived together all this time,

and we did not know.

There is power in

knowing.

There is power in

knowing why you came

to be.

We have not forgotten

you.

We have been gathering

our strength for the

hardest fight of all ~

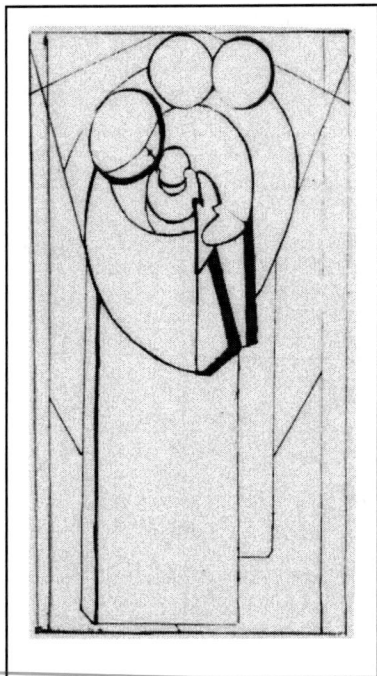

The toughest struggle we will face.

We see you.

We have not forgotten.

We remember ~

And we will live.

And a little child shall lead them.

Is there a child among us

who has any strength left

to take over the lead?

Is there a child among us,

who has room in her heart for hope?

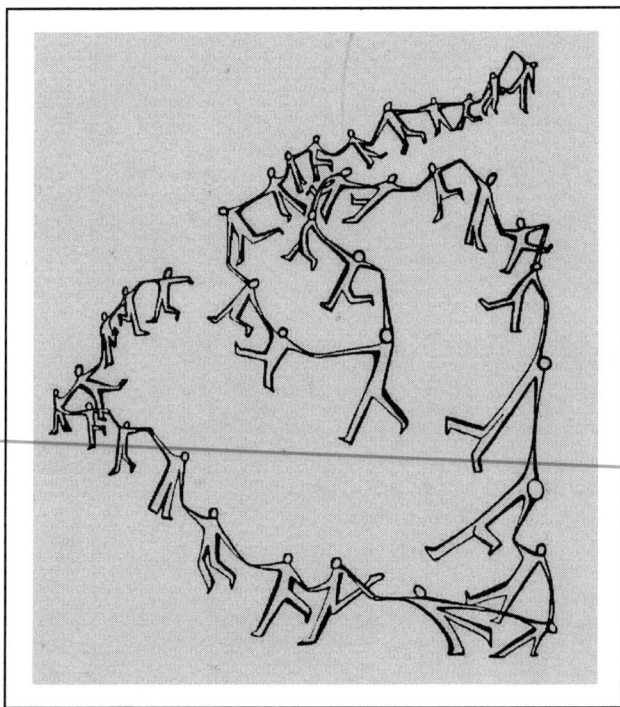

With power and fury that comes from knowledge,

You protect all children small and grown.

You stayed,

Mother of

Mothers.

You lived it.

Your body,

Our body.

No one knew.

You protected

us well.

You allowed us

to leave.

You stayed behind. You felt the pain.

You knew the terror of pain to come.

You carried that.

A child protecting a child.

A child grown, protecting us still.

There is rocking. Thumb sucking.
No words coming. Only pictures.
A child. A baby. A bigger child.

Comfort the child.
Hold the child.
Speak softly to the child.

This child can never be held
enough.

This emptiness cannot be
filled in this lifetime.

This loss will be with us till
eternity.

We hold you and rock you.
Speak softly words of love
and comfort.

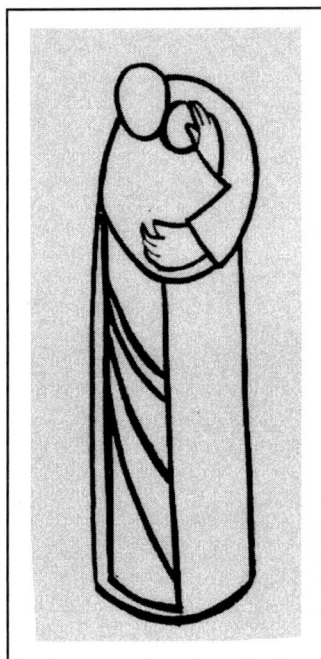

You will have what you need. Needed then.
Need now.

All I can give to another I give to you.

To myself.
To the child who hums ~
Who rocks herself to sleep.

We don't know yet how to do it.
How to live now that all the cutting open is done,
and our insides are on the outside.
We know we can't stuff it back inside,
like it never was.

It has to be out.
People have to see.
I have to see and look and cry and hurt.

Someone will say what to do next
with all that stuff that came from inside me.

We don't have to be dead.

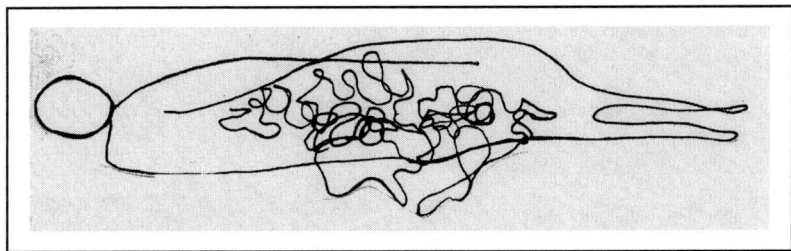

How to be good to Judy:

Listen to all parts of the mind.
See, and say what you see.
Let her rest ~ she works hard.
Check things out with someone we trust ~
someone wise.

We are all important.

We have to be
good to all
parts of the
mind...

Take care of
all parts of
the mind.

Be safe.

Everybody
must rest.

Everybody must be safe.

Remember this.

Do you want to see the baby?

You can touch her.

She is ours.

Isn't she beautiful?

She is real.

We will love her.

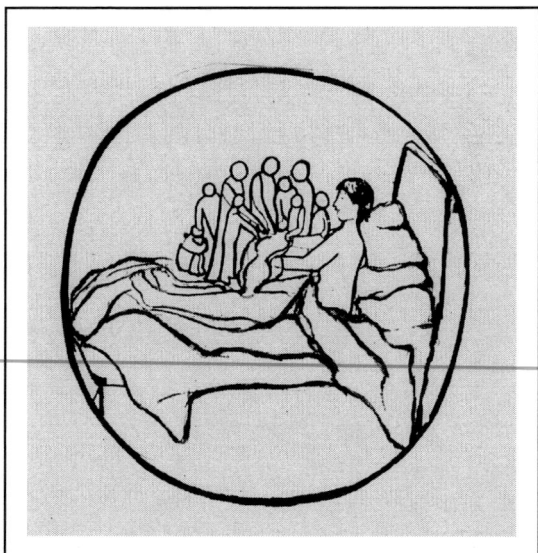

ARE YOU ALRIGHT?

-Who do you ask?

THE SAD ONE. A SAD JUDY. SHE'S CRYING ALONE.
I SEE HER.

-Can you tell her you see her, and she is <u>not</u>
alone?

OKAY. THE GOOD
PART IS, SO MANY
ARE INSIDE.
EVERYBODY KNOWS
ABOUT EVERYBODY
ELSE.
NOBODY IS ALONE.
I SEE YOU.
I CAN TOUCH YOU.
YOU CAN BE SAD,
BUT YOU WILL NEVER
HAVE TO BE ALONE
AND SAD AGAIN.
DID YOU THINK YOU
WERE THE ONLY ONE?
THE SECRETS GOT TOLD. DID YOU KNOW THAT?
BIG PEOPLE KNOW OUTSIDE WHO CAN HELP US
NOW.
EVERYBODY KNOWS WHY WE GOT SO SAD.
IT WAS A SAD THING.
I'M GLAD THEY KNOW. I'M GLAD I FOUND YOU
TODAY ~ ALL ALONE AND SAD, AND I COULD TELL
YOU THE GOOD PARTS.

Oh, Great Mother ~

We are not so brave.

We are small, and alone.

Be with us and we can do wondrous things.

We are many.

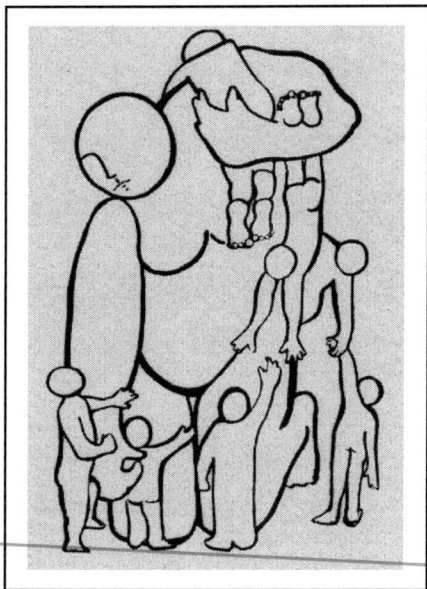

Together with you

we are bigger

and stronger than

any fire you can

imagine.

This flame will grow

within us and shine

through us.

The glow will warm the world,

and they will know us by our love.

I need to heal my soul,
Find my strength,
My spirit,
The part of me that lives.

We would like to draw something strong,
loving, growing.

Something Renee' said ~
"Per aspera, ad astrum."

Through hardship to the stars.

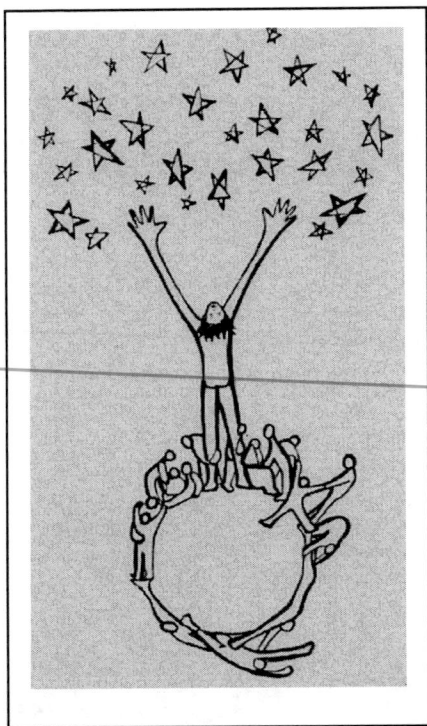

If I had a baby I could love it right.

If I had a baby it would not be sad because it hurt,

or did not understand.

If I was a mommy,

I would know a baby needs to be looked at with

eyes that love.

The mommy loves the baby.

That's all.

Simple.

A simple thing.

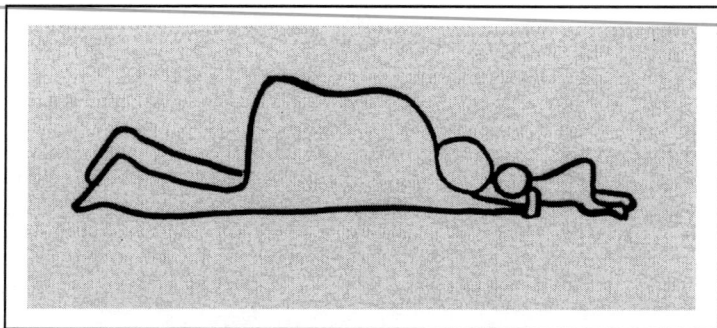

I set me on fire.
Then you will know
How much it hurts
To live with this.

The fire is up to the sky.
The flames rise to heaven.
The angels know,
and see,
and say~

Oh, Child, how you must
hurt.
I am so sorry.
So much pain.
So sad.
So alone.
I see.

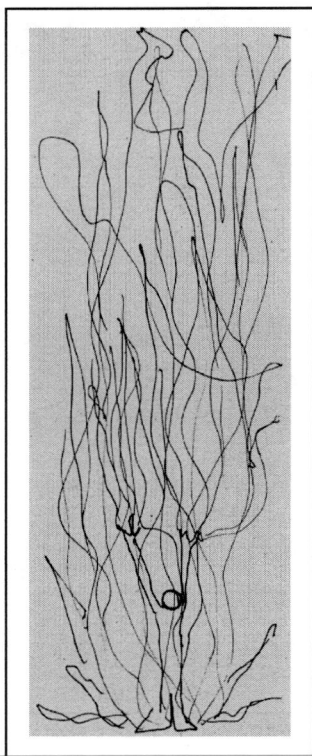

I am with you.

You are not alone.

I see.

I am Gabriel.
You need not be afraid of the truth.
Now there is light.

You need not walk in
darkness alone.

Child Who Walks in
Darkness,
you walk also in fear.

You run from knowing,
and you have always
known.

I will hold you in my
great arms.
I will lift you into the light of truth,
and it will warm you.

The light is good and we are many.

Child, feel the warmth of the light upon your face.
Let it calm your heart, let it take your fears.

In the light of truth, we can see each other, and
none of us will run from the scary truth again.

Life is very hard sometimes.

Maybe tomorrow I'll work on the glass.

I know it's time to do the art again.

Somehow it's time.

We begin again.

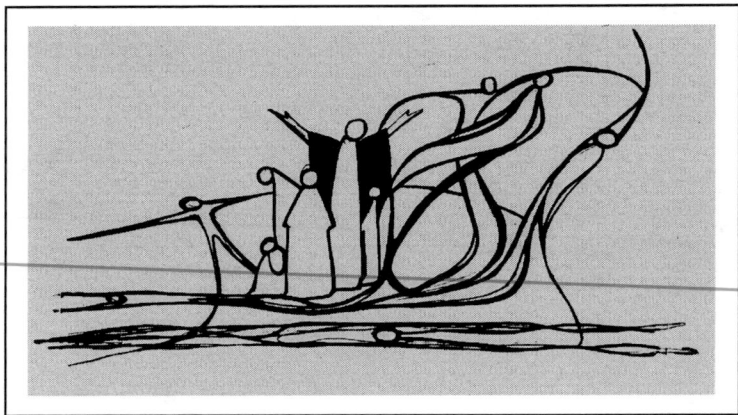

18

The knowing is so big, and so heavy,

It will take all of us to carry the weight.

We share the knowing. Share the feelings.

Together we lift them up off our shoulders~

off our backs ~ off our heart.

Behind the bigness of the knowing ~

the bigness of the feelings ~

we can almost see the beginning of a new day.

The sun is rising.

Good morning all.

This journey has just
begun.
Everything we knew is
gone.

We begin from the
beginning.

We are not happy.

We do not understand.

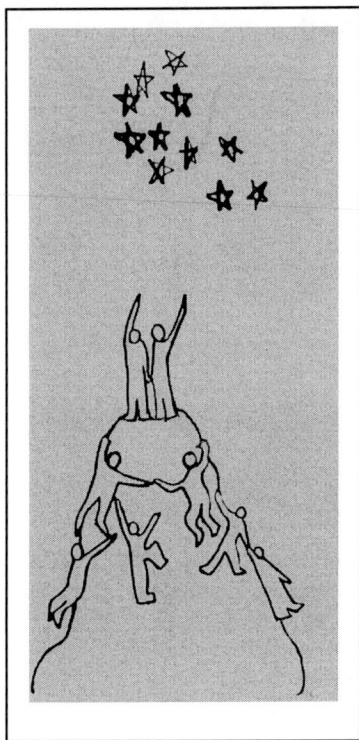

Just keep on climbing, I guess.

Climbing the mashed potato mountain.

20

We live in anticipation still of explosions that
shake us, and wake us from our sleep ~ steal
away our peaceful days ~ our restful nights.

Today is full
of waiting and
hiding behind
corners.
Waiting for
explosions
that come in
dreams
to rock us
awake,
to keep us
unbalanced,
to take away
our living joy.

I read some of my letters in the basement today.

They were very hard to read~ and sad.

There were years of desperation and aloneness~

Of feeling

unloved and

abandoned.

All the

questions...

About

setting us on

fire,

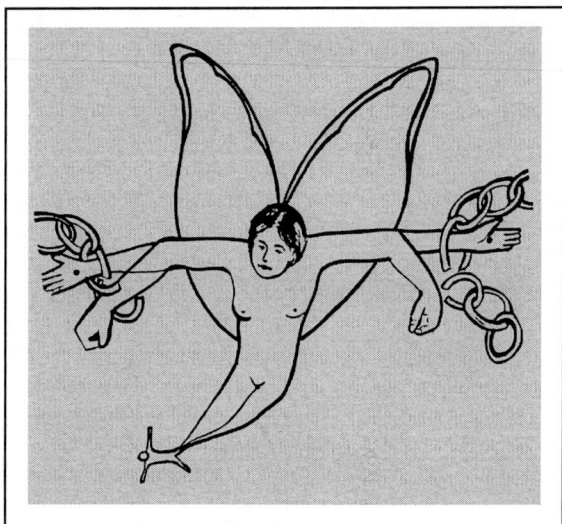

and a fork hitting me in the eye ~

a review in Variety written after a concert

on a thee-hour pass from the hospital

with a bruised hand ~

and the transformation that happened

when I began to sing about Love

and Lunacy.

We are big enough to hold you

and keep you safe ~

One at a time,

and all at once.

We will listen

and protect

and hear

and see.

We will be all

we need to be ~

for each of us

and all of us.

We are

doing it now.

We will Live

and be Happy

and Whole.

We are so Everything.

I am feeling lonely today, thinking about things.

Lonely and little and sad.

It was very mixed up when we were little.

No wonder it's mixed up now sometimes.

No wonder.

The wonder is

I still care.

I still want to live.

Need to be.

The wonder is my

heart can love.

Can trust love.

What can we draw

today?

The Wonder of it All.

24

Deep within the heart is a place where

my child

finds the love

she never

trusted to be

real.

Within my

heart

my child is

loved.

Within my

heart my child

is healed.

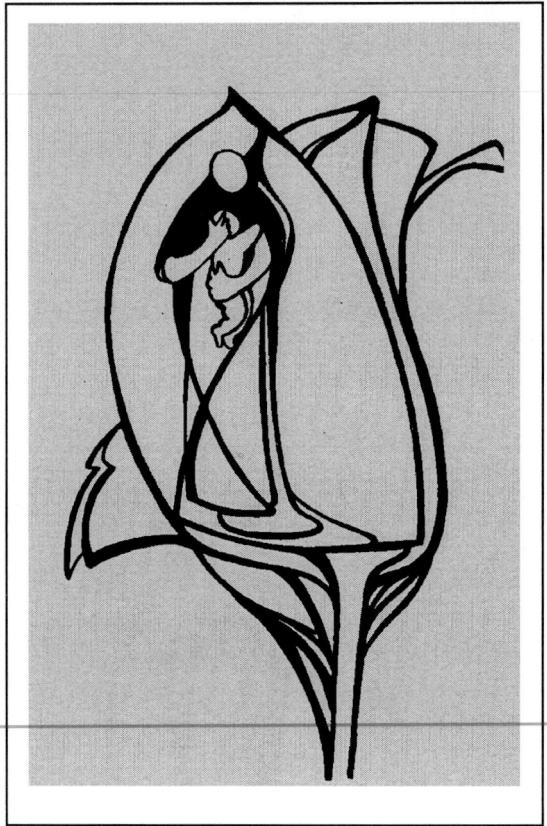

As the child is healed ~

So also is my heart.

Big Judy comforting the child ~ 2 years old.
So sad.

Allow her to cry.
To grieve.

The heart must
heal.

We will all cry
for the hurt in the
heart.

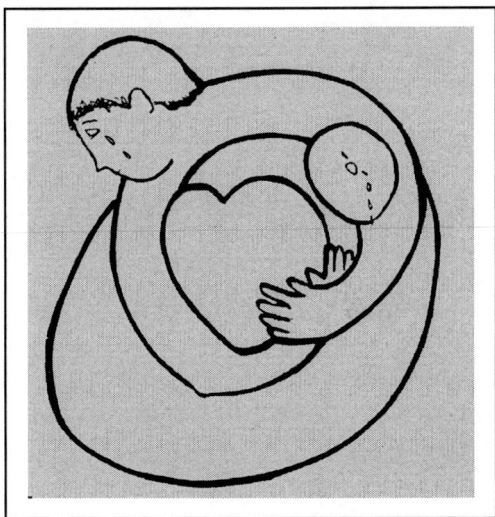

Rock my child
in my arms.
We cry.
Let them cry ~ and cry with them.
Feel the sad. The loss. The alone. The sorrow.

Cry for what was ~ and what never was.
What should have been ~ and could never be.
Cry. Weep. And feel the sad.
Hold each other.
Feel the touching
and the loving in the presence of the sorrow we
share ~ The tears we share.

They are shared tears.

26

We will hold you Little Ones.

We will hold you until the sad is just a memory.

We will love you and protect you.

The world will not hurt you as long as you are in

my arms.

And my arms are
always around you.
Always holding
you.

Know that you are
safe here.
Know that you are
not a child alone
and unprotected.

You are a child loved from within and without ~
and you are safe ~
forever.

~ 27 ~

-WHO OF US IS STRONG?

We mostly all are.

Our body is bigger

and we are stronger

than

all monsters

living and dead.

Dead or alive.

And we are alive.

Big time.

Hooray!

Amen.

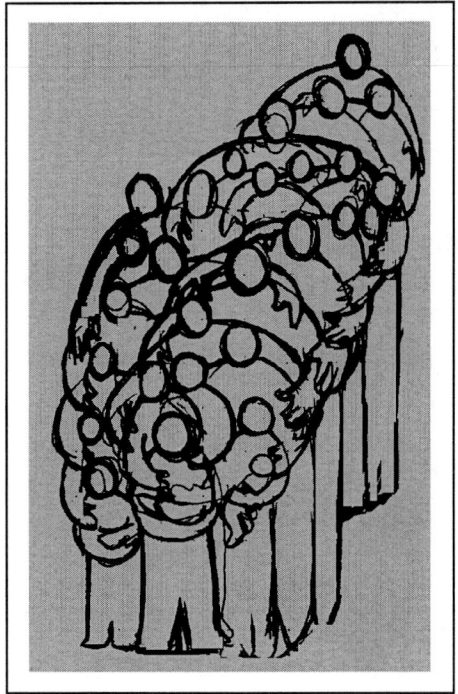

28

This is me who can rock you

and make it feel better.

I hold you tight to me and rock to your rhythm.

The child in me needs to rock.

We are so small.

Such a little thing,

to rock a small child ~

to comfort the child we are.

Such a little thing,

to say ~

I love you.

I see you.

I will help you.

Let me hold you.

I rock you now for all those times that were,

and will be ~

when to be rocked

is to be healed.

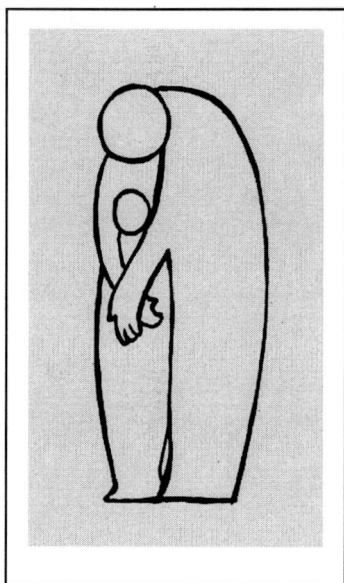

29

This is me, Judy,
who saw in her friends what was in us,
and could give it away.
In giving we receive.
In seeing the need in others,
we see the need in ourselves.

We are all children who
need.
We must be allowed to be
who we are, and what we
cannot be, must be okay.

We will heal our brokenness.
Love the unloved and
unlovable.

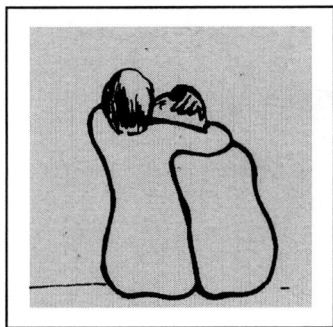

We will hold and rock and stroke the hair, the
worried brow of the child who is me.

We are not so adult that we are without child ~
without the needs of a child. We will give to the
children what they most need...

To be safe. To be loved. To be protected and cared
for and seen and heard and listened to and
watched and held and laughed with and smiled at
with loving eyes, and touched by hands that
caress and do not hurt.

30

Judy is my name.

I know who I am.

I work.

I am an artist.

This is me.

Standing up straight.

Arms open to the world.

Whatever it would give me.

Feet on the floor.

I am strong.

Big.

Tough.

You can't beat me.

Nobody

can kill me.

Nobody can hurt me.

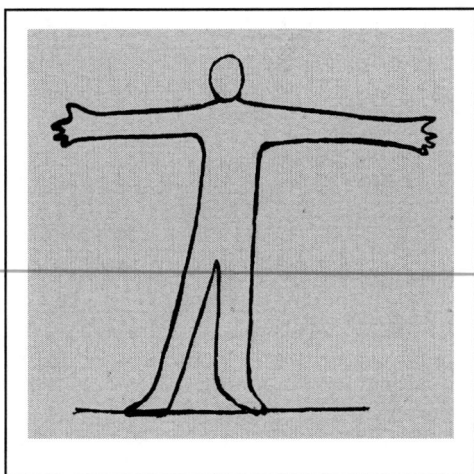

We worry.

Someone big should protect us.

It needs to be somebody inside.

We will win.

I am trying as hard

as I can

to fight

to make it happen.

We know how to

fight hard.

Big Ones up front.

The seed that grows to stalk

and stem and leaf and petal,

That grows toward the light

after a winter sleep.

The warm gentle air that

breathes life

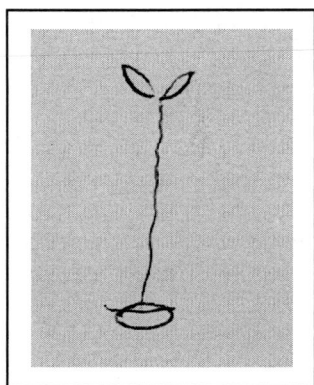

into the seed buried

deep in the earth,

fed by spring rain

that comes for its own sake ~

It all goes on,

in spite of my best efforts

to _not_ see the light,

to _not_ feel the warmth,

to stay dry

and untouched

by the rain.

I got no legs.

I got no eyes.

No ears.

Someone hold me.

Find me.

I am lost.

Falling.

Such a long way to go ~ and up.

A hard climb.

I have been here before.

It looks the same from down here.

One mountain the same as the last.

One hole the same as the next.

I have been here a long time in this hole.

Or maybe it's just one more hole,

just like the last hole.

It always feels alone to be in a hole.

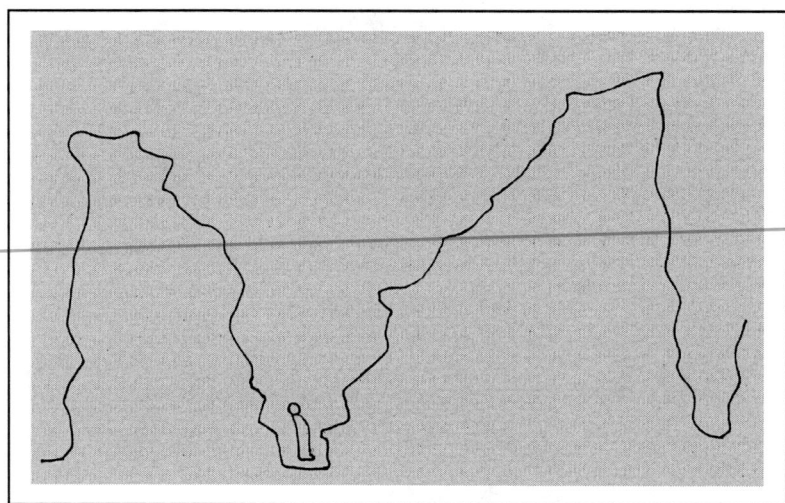

35

We have a need.
A need that we ourselves must fill.

It is a large need ~
But we are many.
Shovels for all of us.

Fill the need.

Bury the monster.
The pain.
The hunger.
The Sorrow.

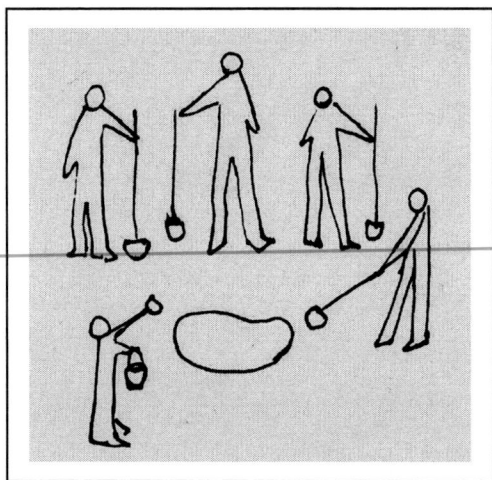

Plant seeds.

Watch them grow.

Add water.

Light.

Tickle softly.

Enjoy.

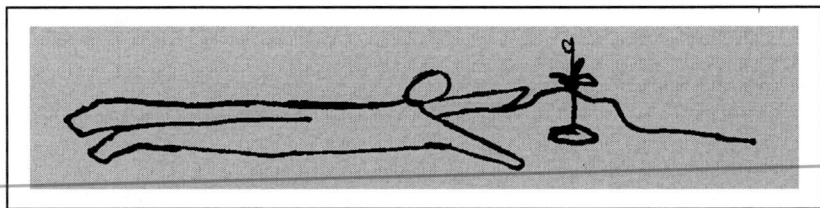

One more wall.
Head on into a brick wall.
Above ~ a dark cloud.

You don't have the energy to look up to see it.
You know it's there.

You know how high the wall is ~
You've seen this wall before.
You can't look backward.
You know what came before.

Ahead is the certainty of more brick walls.
And the cloud.
Ominous.
Bad time for the cloud.

A little light might have been nice ~
with all those brick walls to deal with.

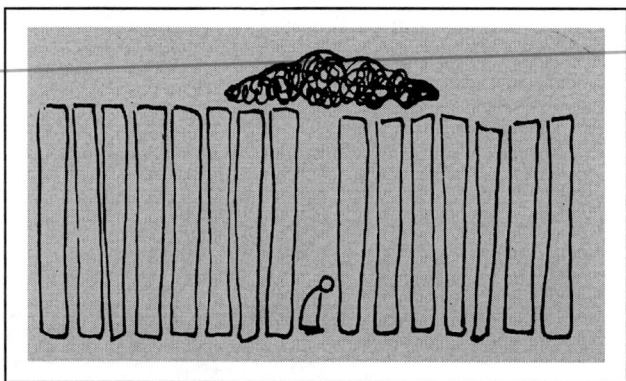

38

Spring

Bursting from the earth into the light that is life-giving.

We are born in a hole in the ground ~

Buried deep ~ a long cold winter.

Soon there will be blossoms and color and fragrance.

People will see and admire and touch and smile.

They will be touched in their heart by one of God's miracles.

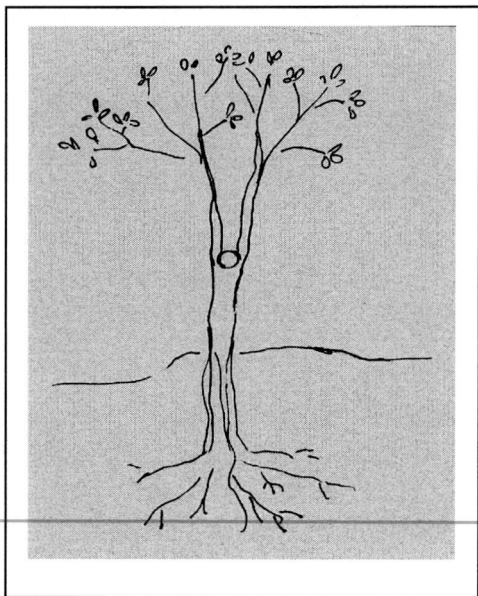

Spring.

New Life.

A chance to show the world what was there always.

Buried deep in a hole.

Waiting.

39

Hello.

I want to say, Hello.

I think there are a lot of sad ones,

and mad ones.

And some of

them have to

yell...

LOOK AT ME!

SEE ME!

LOOK

AT

ME!

That's what

they should do

and yell it

REAL,

REAL LOUD.

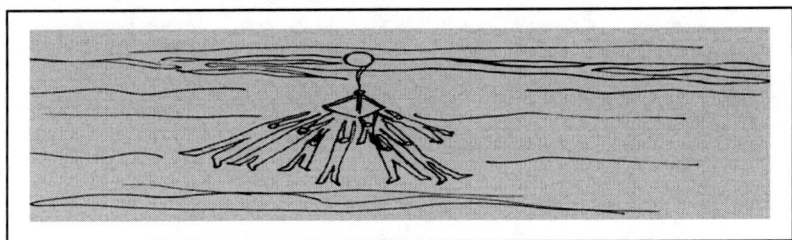

40

I release you from the weight of the sadness.
I release you from the burden of the truth.

It is not yours alone to carry.
I carry you.

I lift you up, and the weight has no substance.
It floats to the top of the water like a balloon.

The sorrow is still there, the sadness, the truth.
But they will not pull you down.
They will not keep you drowning.
We lift, we carry the weight that would hold you
under the water.

Many hands, little and big, hold the weight and
make it light as air itself.

You breathe the air ~ Clean and light ~
pure and fresh.
This is the life giving air we need.
This is the air we were meant to breathe.

Air ~ Breathe now.

41

I will carry you.

I will walk with you

In my arms ~

Up and out of the

water.

Death will not take

you.

The water will not

have you.

You are mine.

We will live.

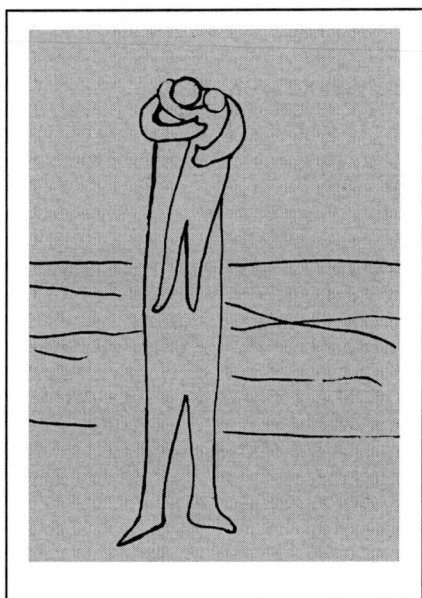

The world is too big.

I am too scared to
be in the world.
Everyone sees me.
I cannot look at
them.

I have no legs that
work.
My hands hold
one-the-other.

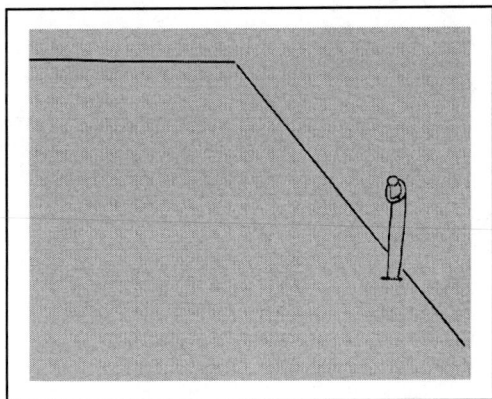

Standing up against the wall, my eyes looking
down. They see nothing. I hear everything.
Waiting.
Afraid to move ~
To be noticed ~
To be talked to.

I will disappear. Gone.
I do not belong in this room,
in this world with other people.
They see inside me.
They know my thoughts ~
Know my secrets before I do.

I say nothing.

Gone.

.

43

This is our heart ~ so full of love.

We could not love us more ~
or appreciate us more.

Our capacity for
understanding,
growing,
caring,
tolerance.

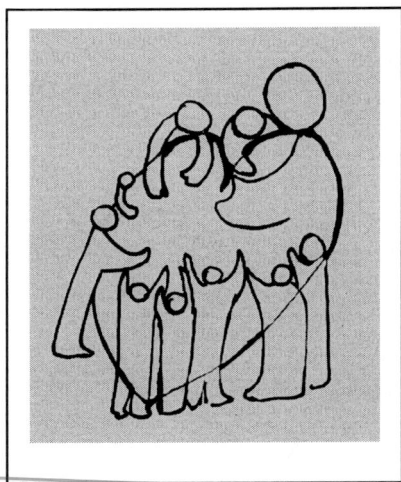

Our desire-to live ~
Our love of others ~
Our ability to go on,
in spite of all that was.

God how we love life.

44

There are some of us who stand together
who want to say, Hello.
They want the world to see we're happy. Together.

-THE WORLD?
One's who don't know
about multiples. We
want to say, We're
here... Inside.
We look like this...
we have smiles though.
You don't see them,
but we can, now.
See, we're waving,
Hello.

-YOU'RE FRIENDLY.
Yes. We like to have friends. We like people.

-BIG PEOPLE?
Sure, any kind that are nice.
Kids too, and our cat, Grable.
And dogs. Anybody's dog.

-WHAT ELSE SHOULD PEOPLE KNOW ABOUT YOU?
They should know we're nice. We didn't hurt
anybody.

-THAT'S WHAT NICE IS?
Yeah. A lot of it.

45

Soon it is Christmas.
The Happy, Merry Christmas.
We've come to
see the baby.
Child of God.
Born to Mary.
We have our
own.
We are Mother
and Father and
Shepherd and
King.
Angel and
Protector.

Behold, a child is born unto you.
The child is the gift He gave us.
His own precious child.
We are given our children whom we love and hold
and teach and grow up right.
Our children are loved without hurt or pain or sex
or rage.

With kindness and caring and thoughtfulness
and the utmost love, we grow them up.
All are welcome. All are gift.
Blessed.

The gift of a child.

~ 46 ~

We are not invisible.

We each have

a voice

Which speaks the truth.

We will be seen,

And heard,

And believed.

47

In the beginning when it was dark ~

we were alone.

In the end we will

be strong ~

Stronger than

silence.

We will be big ~ Bigger than secrets.

We are many ~ More than an army.

We count on it. Strength in numbers.

We will speak it ~ they will listen.

We will be heard ~ they will believe.

They will see ~ we will be seen.

We will belong ~ we will be loved.

And we will love ~ love will come easy.

We will ask and we will receive.

We will give and we will be giving.

And in the end we will live.

And in the end we will be more than we dream.

48

-DO YOU LOVE ME, MOMMY?
I will always love you, Judy Girl.
I will never hurt you.
I would never let
anyone else hurt you.
I will take care of
you.
Grow you up with so
much love you will
never have to wonder
or ask.

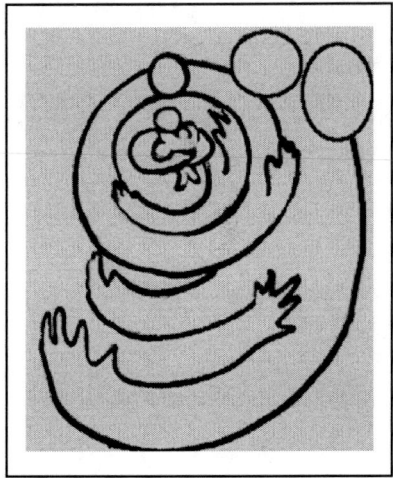

-ARE YOU MY
MOMMY?
I am big enough to love you like you need.
Like you needed from your Mommy.

-WHO ARE YOU REALLY?
I am Judy ~ a Big Judy.
There are many more of us.
We all will take care of you.
It will go better this time.
We know more. We are stronger. And smarter.
And we know people who can help.
The secrets are told. Nothing bad can happen.

-I LOVE YOU, MOMMY.
I love you, Judy Girl.

49

We want to draw thank you ~

To everybody that helped us,

Loved us, along the way.

Some of us who never

smiled

now smile ~

who never spoke,

now speak ~

who never laughed,

now laugh.

Some of us who were

never loved,

now know love.

All of us heal.

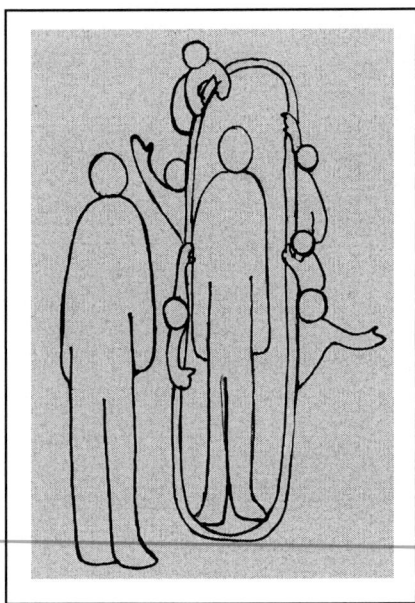

The problem was that no one saw.

No one saw when the plastic bag was there the first time.

I lived it again.

I pulled the bag off my head.

Scratched my neck.

I could breathe again.

I could see again.

I was not alone.

Someone saw~

And did not turn away.

I tried to find you.

I tried to feel you in my life.

I offered myself.

My arms reached to

hold you,

to caress you,

to draw you near.

You were nothing.

You were not there.

Smoke was there.

And air.

My arms fought

harder to feel your

presence.

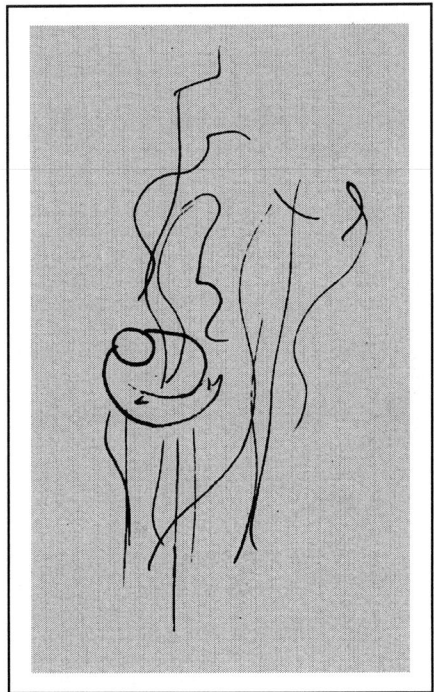

And wrapping tighter, pulling inward,

I found that I had wrapped my arms around

myself. As if to comfort. As if to hold.

As if to recognize, it is my own self

I choose to love.

I wish you well on your journey.

~Judy

EPILOGUE

AN OPEN LETTER FROM THE AUTHOR

a

Thank you for allowing me to share my journey with you. I have received hundreds of e-mails from multiples who visit my website: www.multiple-personality.com

People often ask for guidance. I tell them to look inside, and to journal with passion. Journaling made the difference in my recovery. They tell me that they have tried journaling and failed. They say that they are recording what happens in their day, but they don't find it useful. Or they say that they're afraid of what they'll find, so they never really get started.

With this second edition of *Looking Inside*, I am including some notes on journaling, my journaling philosophy, some of my methods, how I use journaling, and why. I am hopeful that my experience with journaling will be useful to you in your journey toward healing.

As in all things, take what you need, and leave the rest. Those of you who may not be multiple, can apply these same thoughts to your own journaling, and your own healing journey.

WHY JOURNAL?

Journaling was one thing that made the difference in my healing process. And, it is a process. Healing from childhood trauma is an ongoing, life-long process, and it can't be rushed, or hurried. It will take it's own time. You will have to be where you are in your healing until you move beyond, and into something new.

Journaling can help you move forward. Journaling with a passion, with a mission is what helped me to heal, and helped me to heal much more quickly than I had hoped. I wanted it to be fast. I wanted it to be done-over. I wanted my life back. I wanted a chance to have all that I dreamed, and hoped, and wished for. I didn't want to wait, and I knew it would mean work.

I made a conscious decision to figure this out... this multiple personality thing. I decided to know me better than any doctor or psychiatrist or therapist ever could. Understanding how my "system" of personalities worked became my priority, my job, however long it might take.

I was determined not to lose any more time to this than I already had. At forty-four years of age, I was starting over. I was going to understand each and every personality, and I would do it by asking questions. I was determined to be the expert on my system of personalities.

I decided that I would not die from MPD. I had survived my childhood, I could survive MPD. I had acting-out parts, and suicidal parts. I had parts that were determined to hurt the body we share. I wanted to know why. I needed to understand. I wanted to live, or at least, a part of me wanted to live. I knew if I was going to make it, I needed to figure this out.

I started my journaling sessions with one question. Usually it was, "Who needs to talk?" Someone almost always answered. When I got an answer, I asked another question. I asked for more information, asked for others to talk about the same thing. I asked simple questions like: "Why?" "Can you explain." "Who else knows about this?"

I wrote in my journals every chance I got. Every moment I could find, I took out my journal, and asked the questions. It was the most important, most valuable thing I could do. I needed the information that other parts of my mind held.

I knew so very little. In the beginning, when the diagnosis was first made, I certainly didn't know the other parts. I only knew a little bit about a few alters. I didn't know how they thought, or why they might feel a particular way. I didn't know their history, their life-experience, or why they came to be, in the first place. I didn't know why they did what they did. I didn't know what their jobs were, how they got them, or how they felt about their jobs. I didn't know how they felt about anything- about me, or the others in the system. I didn't know them, therefore, I didn't know me. I needed to know everything.

HEAL YOUR SELF

You need to understand your self. You need to know all the parts of you and your mind, and know them better than anyone else. Why? Because no one can live well in chaos, or in the dark. It's uncomfortable, and you keep bumping into things that are in your way. You can't really get much done. You can't live the life you want for yourself. You're still broken. Your spirit, your soul, your heart- broken. Somewhere, you want to heal. You understand that you need to heal.

SEE AND DRAW YOUR DREAMS

See yourself, as you wish to be. Even if it is not real yet, picture your inside people as a harmonious group. Why? Because what we see is real. We can create a better world for ourselves, if we can see it. Visualize it. Picture it in your mind's eye, and draw what you see.

Sometimes, words aren't enough. We know about memories that we can't lose. Flashbacks of things we would rather not see. Pictures we can't escape. We know how real they are. There is a time for drawing those as well, to get them outside where they can be dealt with.

But, the other side of those horrors, are pictures that give us hope, that make us stronger, that bring us together, that allow us to touch and see and feel our selves together, as one. Working, holding, laughing, playing together. Many of the drawings in this book are "wish drawings." I drew what I wished for, and made it real.

I wanted my parts to touch, and hold each other, so I drew that. I wished that the hateful ones, the angry ones, would be loving towards the children and not frighten them. So, I drew them holding the child parts, relating to them in loving ways. My intention was that all parts of the mind would stand together, and work together. I drew exactly that. If your parts understand that your intention is to use your journals to heal, they will respond, and you will all heal. Intention is everything.

Peaceful and joyful pictures will bring you joy and peace. They will replace the painful pictures in your head. These loving pictures of life inside, will be a comfort to you, offer you a peaceful place to rest. They will affirm for you, your very existence, your importance as one person with many parts, and the importance of each of your parts.

I encourage you to picture in your mind, and then draw the wondrous sides of multiplicity, to make these pictures, and the feelings that go with them, more real. Draw strength, cooperation, harmony, and peace, even before you feel them. Feel and draw. Draw and feel.

The pain is inside, and the chaos, and the sorrow, and the joy, and the innocence, and the strength. The healing happens inside. Ultimately you will heal yourself, and you will heal from the inside out.

If you are lucky, you may have help from the outside-friends, therapists, doctors, spouses, and support people who know about dissociation, DID, and MPD. Not all multiples have outside helpers. But all multiples have inside parts who can, and must be part of the healing. In the end, no one can heal you but yourself. Thankfully, you will not be alone in your journey.

Asking and answering the questions will help you know all parts of your mind. Of course, I don't know you. But this is what worked for me, and I am confident it will work for you. Ask the questions with the expectation of getting answers that will help all of you to heal. Don't judge the answers. You simply want the information.

Ask, "Who needs to talk?" "Explain, please." "Say more." "I don't understand yet, can you try to explain again." "Who else knows about this?

Questions like these will help you enormously, and will move you forward quickly. Don't settle for the easy answers. Go deeper. Get input from other parts. Keep asking questions and expect good answers. You will have to explain this kind of journaling to parts that are uncertain of the process. Do your explaining in your journals. If you gently insist that they give it a good try, they will.

Remember that ALL are welcome. Every part of the mind is important to the whole- even parts that we don't particularly like, or parts that are destructive.

As you go further into your healing process, you may discover that the personalities that cause you the most pain, and the most hurt, are the very parts that need the most love. Often, those personalities are the ones that lived through, and were present during the abuse in childhood, and allowed the rest of you to escape.

The parts that yell at you, and berate you, and try to hurt you the most, are often trying, in their own way, to protect you. They have not caught up to the present, and they are using things they learned in childhood, to try to keep you safe. You need to understand why your parts behave the way they do.

Sometimes, personalities that act out, or hurt the body that you share, want to be seen, or want their pain to be seen. They may still feel the hurt of childhood, and they want it to stop. They may be stuck in the invisibility of child abuse. They are often asking that someone see them, and make the hurting stop. You need to know if this is the case. Tell them that you want to know, that you want to see them. Acknowledge them and their pain in your journals.

If you understand why they do what they do, and if you understand how they think, you can intervene. You will recognize their "mistaken thinking", and begin to re-educate them. Some parts may need a new job description, a job that makes sense in the present. There may be other things that they can do to protect you now, or to get the help you need. Together you will figure it out.

As your journaling progresses, you will know when certain personalities are still stuck in the past, and you can help them to get grounded in the present. You will

j

be able to assure them that in the present, they are safe. You will know when child alters are not feeling safe, and you will be able to get them to safety.

You will learn to ask others inside for help. You will learn to form committees to talk to parts that are not being helpful. You will ask others to explain what you yourself cannot explain. You will work together for the good of the whole.

In your journal, you will want to thank the parts of you who kept you alive, the parts that allowed you to escape, the parts that tried and failed, the parts that bear the sorrow, that bear the scars, that feel the pain in the present. Thank those that carry the sadness, and the children who needed only love. They still need your love, and, you will love them all.

All of these things will heal you. If one part starts to heal, all parts will benefit.

LOVE YOUR SELF

You will find a way to love each part of you, and love them back to the whole. I am not talking about "integration." I am talking about loving, unconditionally, each and every part of you.

k

This does not mean that you accept behavior that is unacceptable, or behavior that goes against your goals, endangers your body, is hurtful to others, or puts you at risk. It means that you will love all parts of you in spite of what they do and say, and in spite of the trouble they cause. You will love them, and ask them to change based upon an understanding of who they are, and why they think, feel, and act as they do.

You will work together to change the behavior, change the mind, change the attitude, and purpose of the parts that are working against you. Ask "all parts of the mind" for their help, and you will get help. Work together for the common good. Ask all parts to cooperate.

You will be the Great Mediator. You will learn to work in committee, to form alliances. You will establish common goals. You will make group decisions. You will be able to make informed decisions. Change will happen. Healing will happen.

LOVE

You feel empty inside. You'll never fill the emptiness from the outside. You must begin filling that emptiness from the inside. It's your emptiness. You can fill it.

If unconditional love comes to you from the outside, then you are lucky. But it's your job, your goal, your mission to love YOU better, and more completely, than anyone outside of you ever can.

Love heals... love that doesn't hurt, that has no price, that's easy to understand, and that's given freely with no expectations. This is the kind of love you needed in childhood and didn't get. This is the kind of love you need now.

What you didn't get in childhood you can give to yourself now. Only you can give it to you. You may get love from others, but you won't feel it unless you get it from you first. You won't trust it. You wont believe it. It won't count. It will not matter if the rest of the world loves you, if you don't love you. Start a loving dialog in your journals.

A JOURNEY OF FAITH

It's good to know that you are not alone, that others have gone before. I hope that using these techniques will move you along your path in a way that serves you, and in a way that supports you on your journey. It is my hope that you will find something here that will make sense in your life, and something that will work for you.

We have so little trust, and I am asking you to trust. I am asking you to trust beyond your own self, beyond your own memories, beyond your own experience. I am asking you to trust from a place deep inside, before the hurting began. I am asking you to trust from a place of innocence, and peace, and beauty. Go there and find that peace that is rightfully yours. Rest there a moment before you begin. Then begin journaling.

Trust that this healing journey is the path you are supposed to be on. You are on your way to the center of the Universe, your true beginning. It is my belief that the energy of the Universe flows into, and through, each and every living cell, of each and every living thing. It is divine, and holy, and therefore, so are you. It is the same energy that connects us, you and me. This is our connection.

This is not an easy journey. But it is your journey. You would do well to live in each moment, to breath in and out, and feel the life-force fill you.

I ask you to trust. Trust the process. Trust your own self. Trust that the Universe will support you. Trust that you were meant to live, or you would have been dead long ago. Trust that you are worthy. Trust that you are a living miracle. Trust that your soul is connected, in ways we cannot understand, to the very living breathing life-force that is the soul of all things alive, and good, and as such you are the entire Universe. You are that important. You are it. It is you.

THE GIFT

Now I will ask you to journal like your life depends on it. I want you to journal with a vengeance. Journal with passion. I want you to commit to this as you have never committed to any other thing in your life. I want you to save your own life. Give yourself the gift of life. Give yourself the gift of happiness. Give yourself the gift of dreams. Give yourself the gift of love. Love for no reason. Love without fear. This is what I hope for you. I hope that some part of you, wants these things too, and that you will go after them, and work for them.

Just as we can decide the time of our own death, (through suicide, or as the ancient peoples did by walking into the wilderness), we can also decide the time of our own living. We had a bad start, you and I. We almost didn't make it. Am I right? We almost didn't survive. We almost died a dozen times or more. We almost lost... Big Time. But we did NOT lose. We won. We survived, and we are here to say, we are alive- WE WIN.

But it is not enough to be alive. Now we must LIVE. It is not enough to just live. We must LIVE WELL. We will be all that we dream we can be. All there is. It is "in" us. If we think it, it's real. You can't kill thought, energy, dreams. You may think your dreams are lost, dead, gone. This is a mistaken thought. They are still alive in you. Allow them to live.

THANK YOU

Thank you for allowing me to be with you for a short time on your Journey.

This can be an amazingly wondrous time of your life. Allow it to be just that. Allow yourself the luxury of healing from the inside out. Allow yourself the luxury of knowing you, and how your magnificent mind works.

Look inside. Remember your strength. Feel your power. There is strength in numbers. Honor all parts of your system of alters, all parts of your magnificent, creative, and complex mind. They are all you- all parts of the whole. The goal is to achieve wholeness- in whatever form that takes.

If I may paraphrase Maya Angelou, if you don't like the path you're on, step off. Choose another. A lot of this work is about choices. You can choose healing. You can choose to live. Choose to have a good day today, and every day. Choose to be free of the past. Choose to live in the present. Choose to be responsible for your life, your actions, your thoughts, your dreams, your present, and your future.

You can choose to unburden your heart of all that keeps you stuck in the past. You can forgive yourself. You can forgive God, the Life Force, the Universe. You can even choose to forgive the abusers...or not. There are always choices. Always two ways to turn on any given path. If the choices you are making now do not serve you, choose something different.

Make your choices, then take action toward making those choices real. You can change. You can grow. You can be more than you think you can be. You can do more than you think is possible. You are so amazingly everything.

Feel the power within you. Rise to meet it. Allow it to lift you and carry you away from the past, away from the pain, away from all that hurts little children.

We have our history, and we have multiple personalities. Not easy. But everybody has something. Our childhood is not our life. We create our own life, our destiny, when we participate in our own healing.

The first step in moving forward, is taking the first step. Take action. Do something that will move you in the direction of healing. I invite you to journal with passion. Journal like your life depends upon it.

Be well,

Judy